THE DEER STEALERS

W0226104

GEOFFREY VICKERS

THE DEER STEALERS

A TALE OF OLD ENGLAND

EASY · READERS · ER · EASY · READERS

The vocabulary is based on
Salling/Hvid: English-Danish Basic Dictionary
Weis: Grund- und Aufbauwortschatz, Englisch
Thorndike: The Teacher's Word Book
West: A Gereral Service List

EDITORS
Aage Salling
Erik Hvid *Denmark*

ADVISERS
Marja Wuorenheimo *Finland*
Otto Weise *Germany*
G. de Groot *The Netherlands*
Erling Rundstrøm *Norway*
Torkel Nöjd *Sweden*

Cover design: Ib Jørgensen
Illustrations: Oskar Jørgensen

© 1968 by Grafisk Forlag/Aschehoug Dansk Forlag A/S
ISBN Danmark 87-429-7430-5

Printed in Denmark by
Grafisk Institut A/S, Copenhagen

Old Maundy was repairing the thatched roof of their cottage.

The first thing Hugh could remember was the *forest.* Once when old Maundy, his father, was *repairing* the *thatched roof* of their *cottage*, he went up the *ladder*, and as far as his eye could reach he saw only the tops of the trees. The world outside the forest seemed very far away.

---

forest, big wood with wild animals.

You will still find the forest, if you go and look for it; but in those days, two hundred years ago, it was much bigger than it is now, and there were *deer* and other wild animals, and men wilder than they.

Hugh's father was a *woodman*. The cottage had only two rooms and an *attic*, where Hugh slept with his brothers and sisters. The children were happy, playing and walking about in the wood; and though there was little money, there was always enough to eat – most days for dinner a *rabbit* or some kind of bird, and sometimes *meat* which Hugh's father called "forest *mutton*".

When Hugh was ten something very strange happened. He was carrying a big *basket* and looking for *mushrooms* and he had reached a

woodman, a man who cuts down trees in a wood, woodcutter.

attic, room just under the roof of a house.

meat, that part of an animal which you eat; bacon, for example, is meat.

mutton, meat from a sheep.

A swarm of wild bees had settled on the head of the old man.

place in the wood some way from the house when he saw something very strange. An old man was standing there quite still, bent forward, and at his feet lay a *bundle of sticks.* He had a *skin coat* on, which reached nearly to his *knees,* and his arms, which were very long, hung by his sides. But where his head should have been, was something which looked like a big ball that moved all the time.

Hugh went nearer and saw what it was. A swarm of wild *bees* had *settled* on the head of the old man, who was afraid to move for fear that they would sting him to death.

Hugh knew something about bees, and knew that at swarming time many thousands will come together and settle on anything which is handy. Once he had helped his father to put in a *hive* a swarm which had settled near the cottage. He walked up to the man and put his basket on the ground under his face so that the swarm hung over the basket from his long white hair. The man said nothing and did not move while Hugh with two *branches loosened* the ball of bees, which fell into the basket and stayed there.

But the old man did not move till Hugh had got the last bee out of his hair. Then he stepped back and turned his face to Hugh's.

Hugh found himself looking up into two very blue eyes. The man looked from Hugh to the bees and back again and laughed softly.

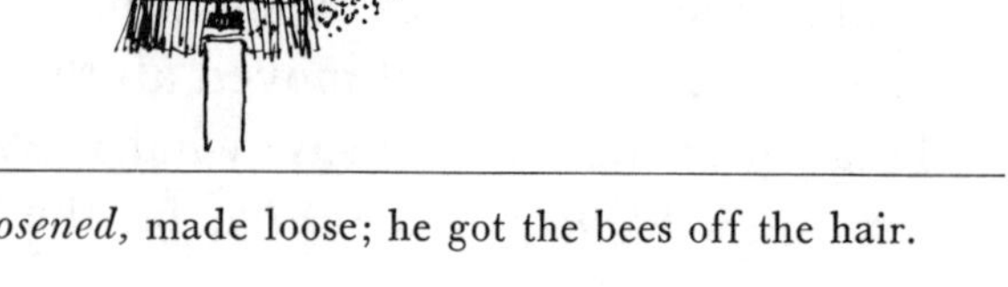

---

loosened, made loose; he got the bees off the hair.

They moved a little farther away and looked at each other.

"I have something to thank you for," said the man. "What is your name, and where do you live?"

When Hugh told him, the man gave a little laugh.

"Is that so?" he said many times. "I have a feeling that we shall meet again, and some day perhaps I shall be able to pay you back for this. But what can I give you now? I know. You can keep the bees."

He took his bundle of wood and was about to go.

"Who are you, please?" asked Hugh.

Something in the blue eyes changed and Hugh found himself suddenly *frightened.* But the man's voice was kind as he answered: "I have many names and I live where I am. But you can call me Pat."

He moved away and in a moment he had *disappeared* in the wood. Hugh ran home, not knowing how much that meeting was to mean to him later on.

---

frightened, filled with fear; very much afraid.

disappeared, gone away so that Hugh could not see him any more.

Hugh and his father came back that night, when the bees were sleepy, and put them in a hive and took them home; but old Maundy was very angry with him.

"You must not walk so far," he said, "or you will find yourself in Dead Man's Bottom, and that will be the end of you."

"What is that?" asked Hugh.

"Somewhere in the forest – I won't tell you where – is a *ravine* with a *stream* through it, and it is called Dead Man's Bottom. Why? Because people who walk about in that part of the forest are found dead in that ravine next day. The people who live in those parts don't like other people."

"Who lives there, father?"

"*Outlaws* and wild men of all sorts. Some of them begin by killing deer and end by killing men. Others begin by killing men and then live by killing deer. You remember my words, let the deer alone, and live poor but *honest*, as your father does. Now don't ask any more questions."

After that, Hugh liked the forest more than

---

outlaws, men who did not live with other people. Anybody who met an outlaw could kill him.

be honest, do nothing wrong.

ever. At first he kept close to the cottage, but soon he was walking farther than before, though very carefully. He wanted to learn his way about the wood, and he always hoped to see Pat again.

He did see him – many times; but always Pat saw him first. He would be lying by a river and a *shadow* would fall on him; and there was Pat standing over him. Or he would be walking among the trees, trying to get close to a *squirrel*, and something would hit him; and there in the branches above him would be Pat. Often he thought that Pat was watching him, but would not show himself.

Whenever they met, Pat would have with him a small bundle of sticks.

The man was a *mystery*. At first Hugh had thought him old because of his white hair; but he did not move like an old man. Once when they were together Pat lay on the ground, and put his arm down a rabbit *hole* and brought up five young rabbits. Hugh saw the little animals lying in his big hand – and he saw his arm. The *skin* was very white, and under the skin, from *wrist* to *elbow* and elbow to *shoulder* were big *muscles*. Pat put the rabbits back and, when he saw the boy looking

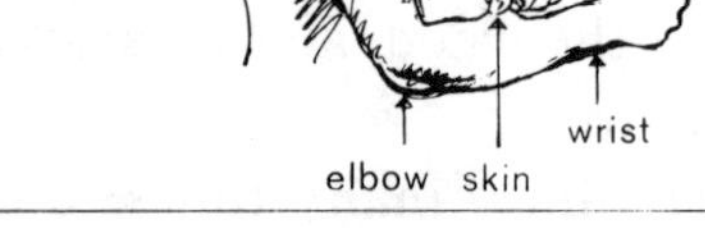

---

mystery, something you cannot understand.

at his arm, smiled and said: "Feel it!" Hugh put his fingers on it; it felt like cold *iron.* Always, when he thought of Pat after that day, he saw that picture – the big white arm and the baby rabbits in the hand.

---

iron, a hard metal; motor-cars are made of iron.

Once, when they were together, Pat stopped and *listened*. Hugh listened too, and he heard the cry of a dog far away.

"What is it?" he asked, but Pat was standing quite still and did not answer. The cry came again, clearer, frightening him, though he did not know why.

"*Bloodhounds*," said Pat.

They stood still and heard the hounds pass to the south of them, and the crying of the hounds die away. Hugh had been too frightened to speak, but now he asked Pat:

"What were they *hunting*?"

"A man," said Pat. There was a hard look on his face, which Hugh had not seen before.

"A man! What do they hunt men for?"

Pat seemed to come to himself. He looked at the boy.

"What for? Why, for killing deer or sheep – or other things. It is the law. But the forest

bloodhound

---

listened, tried to hear.

hunt, run after, look for, try to find.

is deep, full of places where you can hide, and full of good food. So anyone that has the *gallows* waiting for him outside, *takes to the forest.* They cannot find him there; but if they *get* the dogs *on his track*, he can do nothing – if he does not know the way."

"Oh, Pat, do you think the man they were hunting got away?"

Pat smiled a little.

"I know he did. And I heard which way the hounds ran, so I think I know which way the man is going. People who go that way nearly always get away."

He stopped. Then he said slowly:

"You know Wainfleet Bottom? If ever you are hunted by bloodhounds go to the head of it and then run east. Now I have told you a *secret.* Forget it till you need it; and I hope you never will."

takes to the forest, goes to live there.
get on his track, follow or hunt him.
secret, something which nobody must know about.

He changed his tone and went on.

"Yes. Bloodhounds are no fun. Let a bloodhound get the *scent* of a man, even from a piece of his clothes, and it will follow him all night, and find him anywhere. It is poor fun to be hunted by bloodhounds."

"Have you been hunted by bloodhounds, Pat?" asked Hugh. But Pat just smiled.

"I have had a funny life," he said.

That summer Hugh was with Pat for many an hour. Often the man would be *silent* for hours together; at other times he talked of many things, showing Hugh the ways of the wild animals, teaching him to fight, showing him how to find his way in the woods, or telling him long stories, of which Hugh never knew how much to believe. The boy did not tell anyone, not even his father, about these meetings.

One day when Hugh and Pat were walking through the wood, Pat suddenly stopped and pointed. Fifty yards away among the trees stood a fine *stag*. It could not smell them, for

---

scent, smell; if a hound or dog gets the scent of a man, it can follow his track and find him.

silent, not talking.

Pat pulled the string back to his ear.

the wind came towards them. Hugh felt Pat move beside him and looked at him.

From among the bundle of sticks he took out a short, strong *bow* and a long *arrow*. Silently and very quickly he put the *string* on the bow, put the arrow to the string and pulled it back to his ear. The sound of the string when the arrow flew from the bow sang through the forest, and the deer lay dead with the arrow through its heart.

Hugh looked from the deer back to Pat. He had already put the bow back among the sticks, and with his white hair falling on his back he looked like an old man who was looking for sticks for his fire.

"That is how it is done," he said. "The bow is still good for some things."

He put out his great hand and took the boy by the arm.

"Run home, now," he said. "Good-bye. We shall meet again, some day."

When he had gone a little way, Hugh turned round to see what Pat was doing. He saw him walk slowly up to the dead stag. Even he could not believe that it was not an old man he was looking at. Then there came a change. Pat put down the sticks, took the stag and put it on his back, took up the sticks again and moved quickly and silently away among the trees. Almost at once it seemed he had disappeared. Hugh sat down and cried. He knew that it would be a long time before he would see Pat again.

Hugh was sixteen. Nearly every day now

he was with his father working in the forest, *felling* trees, cutting off the branches and putting the *logs* together in *stacks*. Sometimes great *waggons* came from towns outside the

felling, cutting down.

forest, and there were good days putting the heavy logs on the waggons and watching the horses when they pulled the waggons through the forest to the *track.* Sometimes his father set him to work in the forest and left him for the whole day; and what his father did on those days Hugh never knew.

One *autumn* morning Hugh and his father stood in the open place in the forest where they were working. It was early. Everything in the forest was wet and they could smell the dead *leaves.* Long *poles* that they had *trimmed* the week before lay ready to be taken out of the wood. There was also, Hugh saw, some *faggots* which had not been there before. An hour passed before a waggon appeared, drawn by three brown horses. On the *box* sat a big red-faced man, who said to Maundy:

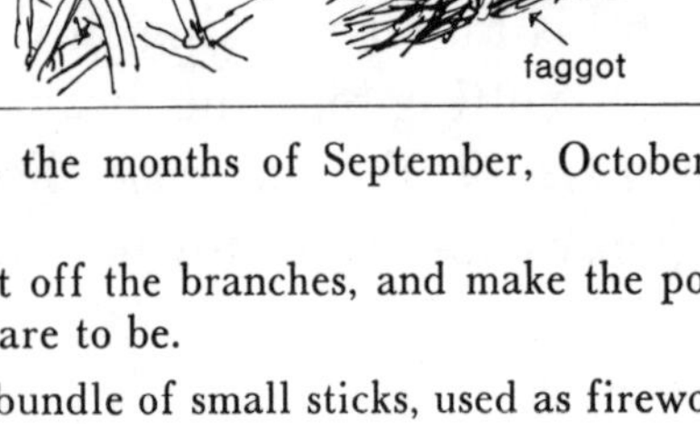

---

autumn, the months of September, October, and November.

trim, cut off the branches, and make the poles as long as they are to be.

faggot, bundle of small sticks, used as firewood.

"Morning, Maundy; we are late. The track is nothing but *mud.* We shall never get back through it with the logs on. You will have to find me another way."

The waggon stopped and he sprang off, looking at Hugh.

"My son," said Maundy. "Pete cut his foot with an *axe* yesterday, so I brought him. He is all right."

"Must begin some time," said the other man, whom Maundy called Perron.

"All the same, I don't like it," his father answered.

"Does he know anything?" asked Perron.

"Nothing yet," said his father.

Maundy and Perron began putting the poles and the faggots on the waggon, and Hugh, as he helped, saw that they were doing it in a very strange way. In the middle they laid the faggots of firewood; at each end they laid some very short logs; and on top of all they laid the long, trimmed poles. Nobody could see the faggots, and anyone who saw

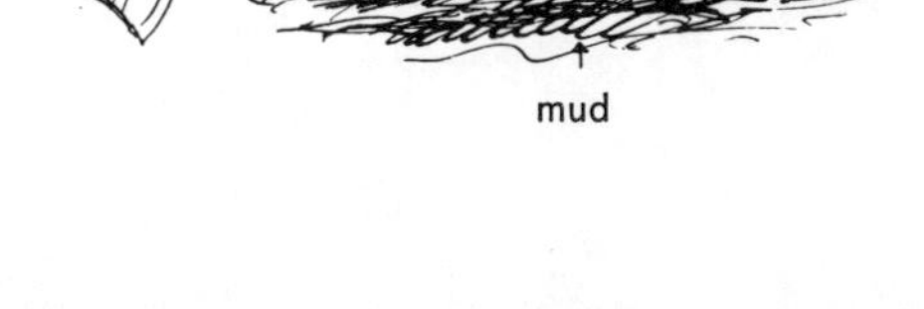

the waggon would think that there were only long poles on it. They worked very fast and did not stop until they had put the last pole on the waggon. Then Perron said:

"I had better get away with it quickly. Can you tell me a better way to the *forester's* house than the way I came? I can't get through the mud with all these poles."

"I could show you one," said Hugh. "May I come?"

The men looked at each other. Maundy said:

"All right, take him all the way if you like and see what you think of him."

Hugh went to the leading horse, Perron got up on the box and took the *whip*. Hugh shouted, the whip *cracked*, and slowly the heavy waggon got through the mud and moved away. When it reached the track, Hugh came up to sit on the box beside Perron and showed him the best way to the forester's house.

The forester walked round the waggon and *counted* the ends of the logs at one end. Then he counted those at the other end.

---

forester, person that helps the man who owns the forest to look after the animals, etc.

count, see how many there are.

"Thirty-two fifteen-foot poles," he said. Perron handed down some money, and they drove away.

Now Hugh saw that the forester had thought that the logs at each end of the waggon were ends of the same poles, and had known nothing of the faggots of firewood in the middle. But he could not understand why

Perron would pay for more poles than he had taken, just to carry away a few faggots of firewood, which he could have got nearer home. But he said nothing about it to Perron, who was very pleased with what he had done.

"Would you like to come all the way to Shaston?" Perron asked when they were out of the forest.

"Oh, yes," said Hugh. He had never been as far as the town, which lay outside the forest, but he had seen it from the top of the hill they were driving towards.

There were few trees now, and open places with *heather*. At last they came out on a *moor* on the top of a hill. As they crossed the top, Hugh saw to the west a beautiful green *valley*, and in front of them, far away, the town of Shaston. A cold wind came over the moor, and on the hills were the blue shadows of sailing *clouds*.

Perron began to talk. He asked Hugh what he could do, and was pleased with his answers. The road turned, and they drove down the hill until at last they reached the valley and drove towards Shaston together with a lot of other waggons.

Everybody knew Mr Perron and he had a word for everyone. Hugh, who had never

seen a town before, sat on the box, looking at the people in the streets and the big houses.

Then there was a crack, and before he knew what was happening Hugh found himself on the road with wood and faggots over him. A *wheel* had come off and the top-heavy waggon had turned over on its side.

Hugh got up, very little hurt. The waggon lay in the middle of the street so that nobody could pass, and already there was a *crowd of people*. Perron was standing on the top of the waggon with the whip in his hand, calling out to people to keep back. He was angry. When he saw Hugh get up, he called him and put the whip in his hand.

My house is in the next street. I must go and get another waggon. You stay here, and whatever you do, let no one take a faggot – see? Keep them away from the poles if you can, but don't let a faggot go! Do you understand?"

Hugh was very frightened. Perron *jumped* down, went up to the horses, which stood quietly in the street, and then called Hugh again. Taking him by the arm, he said in his ear:

"If one of those faggots is taken when I come back, it will be the worse for you!"

Then, leading the horses, he ran up the street.

---

crowd of people, many people together.

jump, spring.

wheel

Hugh stood on the waggon, holding the whip, and looked round at the people, who were laughing at him. The poles and faggots lay between the overturned waggon and the houses. One of the faggots had opened at one end and in it Hugh saw something.

In a minute he had jumped down from the waggon, taken the faggot and begun putting the others on top of it. Before the people saw what he was doing, he had put all the faggots together, and was sitting on them. His heart was beating, because now he knew what he was sitting on.

In every faggot was a piece of *venison.*

"What are you carrying that about for?" said a man.

"Perron's fire has gone out, and he has gone to the forest to get a stick or two," said another, and everyone laughed.

"Give us a faggot," said an old woman, "Perron will never find out."

Hugh said nothing, but raised the whip, and at that the people laughed again and they came nearer. Perron was a *miser* as well as a rich man, and the people thought that it

---

venison, the meat of a deer used as food.

miser, person who loves money and does not spend it.

would be a good idea to take the faggots which he had got from so far away.

"Let us take the faggots," cried someone. "He has never given any firewood away. It is time he began."

"Stand back," said Hugh; but the people only laughed. Then a young man jumped forward, got hold of one end of a faggot and tried to get it out.

In a minute it would open and everybody would see the venison inside. He would have to get that man away, so he dropped the whip and jumped off the top of the faggots right on the man's head. They fell together in the street, while the people, who loved a fight, laughed.

"Good, *lad*! At him, lad! Don't let a baby knock you down, man!" they cried. But before the angry man could get hold of Hugh, he had got back on to the top of the faggots and was keeping the people away with the whip.

The young man he had knocked down got up, and came nearer. Twice Hugh hit him in the face. The third time, the man got hold of the whip and took it from Hugh.

---

lad, boy or young man.

"Now!" he cried, and came towards Hugh.

Hugh took one of the long poles and pushed him down into the street again. He sprang up, and took another pole himself. The others were coming nearer, too. Hugh knew that he could not keep them back any longer, but just then an old man came along, and the people stood back to let him pass. He was moving slowly with one hand on the walls of the houses, holding in the other a stick. It was clear that he was *blind*, for when he felt the wood in his way, he stopped and felt around him with his stick.

"What is happening here?" he cried.

"Look out, old man," said someone. "There is a fight on."

"A fight, is it?" said the man. "Stand clear of me, then, whoever you are." And he began to swing his stick round his head, and in this way he kept the people away from the faggots.

"Here," said a woman. "Stop that! I will lead you round. It is only a waggon which is overturned."

But the old man only began swinging his stick faster.

---

blind, a blind person cannot see.

Hugh took one of the long poles and pushed him down into the street again.

"No, you don't," he cried. "Keep your hands off me."

At that moment Perron came with a new waggon and two or three strong men, who pushed back the people with sticks and began putting the faggots and poles on the waggon. Hugh looked round for the old man. He was not there.

Later, in Perron's house, Hugh told him what had happened. Perron was pleased, but

Hugh could see that he was wondering how much he knew, so he said:

"I know what was in those faggots. I saw, but I don't think anyone else did."

Perron looked at him for a long time without saying anything.

"You know, do you?" he said at last. "Then I think you also know that, if this day's work was known, your father would be *hanged*?"

"My father?"

"Well, of course. He has sent venison out of the forest for years and years. Do you mean to say that you have never eaten any?"

"Was that what it was?" said Hugh, thinking of the "forest mutton".

Perron laughed. "You have lived by *poaching* since you were born," he said. "And now we must do something. You may not have been the only one that saw something today. There was a forester among the people."

"But he can't get at the faggots now, can he?"

"No, but up in the forest there are more, waiting to be taken away tomorrow. He may find out where these faggots came from and

---

be hanged, be sent to the gallows. See picture on page 15.

poach, take deer or other animals which are not yours.

go and have a look. You must get back to your father, lad, tonight, see? You must tell him what has happened. When we *load* to-morrow, there must be no faggots about. If there are, and they come when we are loading, your father will be hanged, and so will you. Do you understand?"

Hugh sat silent and frightened. Perron put his hand on his shoulder.

"You are a good boy," he said. "See here. You shall have something to eat, and sleep a little. Then, as soon as it is dark, you shall start back. If you get through and tell your father, I will see to it that you shall never be sorry that you came with me. I want a boy like you. How would you like to take a job in my *saw-mill* at Blandford? You do not want to live on poaching all your life. I would do something for you because I know your father, but after tonight I will do even more because I know what sort of a boy you are. Now let us find you some food."

And with that he took Hugh to the kitchen.

It was almost dark when Hugh got out of Mr Perron's house and walked down the streets of Shaston. As soon as he was clear of

---

load, put the poles and faggots on the waggon.

saw-mill

the last house he began to run. On the hills before him he could see the beginning of the friendly forest, a dark line, looking very far away.

Perron's last words ran in his head. "If anyone follows you, you will have to get away from them in the forest. Whatever you do, don't lead them home."

He reached the top of the hill. There was the forest. At the track was a forester's house with a light in the window. He passed it, came into the forest, began to run again – and fell *full length* over a *rope* which was *stretched* across the track. Before he could get up, a man was on his back.

"Got him!" a voice said. Two men took him, one by each arm, made him stand up, and took him into the forester's house. There was only one room with a table and a chair on which another man was sitting. A *lantern* on the table gave the only light. The men put him before the table and held him there.

"This is the lad," said one. Hugh remembered that he had seen him in the crowd round the waggon.

Hugh looked round. The door was behind him, and that was the only way out. The man at the table looked at him.

"Answer our questions," he said, "or it will be the worse for you."

Hugh saw that all the men were foresters. He said nothing and waited.

"You were on Perron's waggon today," said the man behind the table. Hugh was silent.

lantern

He fell full length over a rope which was stretched across the track.

At once Hugh struck the man on the bridge of his nose.

"Answer!" said the man, and one of the others *twisted* his arm.

This made Hugh *desperate*. These men would torture him till they killed him or got the whole story out of him, word by word. Anything was better than that. Then he re-

---

twist, turn; what you do when you want to get the water out of a piece of cloth.

desperate, ready to do anything to get free.

membered some of those fighting tricks that old Pat had taught him long ago.

Suddenly he *stamped* as hard as he could with the *heel* of his heavy *boot* on the foot of the man on his left, at the same time driving his head up under the man's *jaw*. The man let go of Hugh's left arm. At once Hugh *struck* the man on his right side on the *bridge of his nose* and drove his left knee into his *stomach*. The man fell back. For a moment Hugh was free. With all his force he took the table in front of him and overturned it on top of the third man. The lantern fell to the floor and went out. He sprang to the door, tried to find the *latch*, found it and opened the door – just too late. A hand took him by the *collar*. He tried desperately to get free, and in the fight his *coat was torn from top to bottom*. The next moment he was running up the track, free.

The three men fell over each other, trying to get out of the door after him. He heard them fall on the road and call out to one another. Two came running after him, but he had a start of them and was faster than they. He ran up the track, then, turned into

---

stamped, put his foot down suddenly and very hard.

the wood, lay down and waited. The angry men knew that they could not get him in the dark. He heard them turn back.

He lay still for a while, till he had got over his *terror*. He was very pleased with himself. If only he could meet Pat again and tell him! Suddenly he felt cold and found that the whole back of his coat was torn away. He got up and went on to get home.

In half an hour he stopped again. He was on well-known ground now, not far from home. It was very dark under the trees, and very still and *silent*. The only thing he could hear was the sound of small drops of water falling on the dead leaves.

Then far behind him he heard the wild *baying* of a dog.

Three times the cry came. Then it stopped, and all was silent again. Hugh walked up to a tree and put his face against the wet *bark*; he felt very sick, because he had heard that cry before, and he knew what it was. There was a bloodhound on his track.

---

terror, great fear.

silent, there were no sounds.

baying, the deep crying of a hound or dog when it is hunting.

Hugh's coat was torn from top to bottom.

The house was only half an hour away, but he could not go there now. The dog had got his scent from the piece of his coat which the forester had torn away; it would lead the men to the very door. Better let the bloodhound take him in the forest than that. But where else could he run?

He thought of that day years ago when he had first heard a bloodhound. He saw again

Pat's face and remembered his words: "Go to the head of Wainfleet Bottom and then east." That was the only thing he could do. Could he find Wainfleet Bottom in the dark? He thought so, and ran on again, keeping to the open parts of the wood where he could

see. Soon the ground began to *slope*; this must be Wainfleet Bottom. There was a *path,* he knew.

He ran down the slope and found it. Here he stopped, took off his *jersey* and put it away in some bushes. Turning north, he ran up the path.

It was dark and silent in the little valley. How long the path was! He ran on and on and at last he came out at the head of the valley. Here he turned right. Ahead of him lay a part of the forest where he had never been.

Suddenly the thought came into his head that even if he got away, what was the use?

He was to tell his father something, and how could he reach his father now? In the morning it would be too late. Perhaps the foresters had given up? He could hear nothing behind him. He almost stopped, and thought of going back the way he had come and make for home.

Then from the valley came the wild baying of the bloodhound, much nearer. It must have found his jersey. The men were close behind him at that very moment while he stood still. He turned east and ran like a rabbit through the trees.

The ground fell away in a long slope, and as he ran down the slope, he heard the hound crying wildly behind him. At the bottom was a stream. He ran through it. Then came another hill covered with trees.

The men were so near now that he could hear running feet behind him, and before he was half-way up the hill he heard men run through the stream behind. Now they were in the wood on the hill; it was a question of moments. At the top of the hill there were still more trees. He ran blindly forward, saw – too late – a *sheer cliff* in front of him, cried out and fell down.

For one moment Hugh felt himself falling,

falling through the wet branches of small trees, down the cliff. Then suddenly he stopped. He was lying on his back on *grass*, his feet in running water. He lay still, *wondering* if he was dead. Then at the top of the cliff he heard the hound. He heard it running along the cliff, trying to find a way down. He heard the men, too. And suddenly it came to him that this must be the place Pat had told him about, the place where he could go to if he was hunted by bloodhounds.

He put his head into the stream; the water was cold as ice. He got up on hands and knees, and found that he could move, and he *crawled* a little way on hands and knees along the stream. Then his knees gave way and he fell down on his face; he could not move another *inch*. And as he lay *hopeless* in the long grass, a hand was put on his shoulder and a voice he knew said:

"Lie still, lad."

"Pat!" he said and began to cry.

For a few moments Pat let him lie there. Then he said: "Drink this!" It was like fire, but he felt stronger for it. And when Pat said,

---

he wondered, he asked himself.

crawl, move along on hands and knees.

inch, about 2.5 cm.

hopeless, without hope.

"Follow me", Hugh found that he was able to crawl.

Pat crawled up the stream till he came to another sheer cliff. Hugh could just see a black hole in it and through that hole the stream ran out. Pat crawled into the stream on hands and knees, right up to the mouth of the hole.

"This," he said to Hugh, "is Dead Man's Bottom; and this is the way out."

And with that he crawled into the hole.

Hugh crawled along the *tunnel*. The water

ran round his hands and knees. The roof was only a few inches over his back. It seemed a long time before he saw light round the body of the man in front of him, and came suddenly into a little valley.

Pat put Hugh down on the grass and felt him all over and put his own coat round him. Then he took him in his arms and Hugh told his story. Pat said nothing until Hugh had told him everything. Then he laughed.

"You are a great lad," he said. "When I saw you push that man down the faggots in Shaston today, I knew you were all right. And then this!"

"You saw me? I did not see you."

"Of course not, lad. You only saw an old blind man."

"Pat! Was that you?"

"Perhaps; there are many things you do not know about me. But we have no time to talk. The first thing is for you to get back and tell your father, while I see to the faggots."

"You?"

"Why, boy, if you had gone to your father first he would have had to come and tell me. It would have taken him more than an hour to get here."

Pat took out two things and gave them to Hugh. They were like big *stockings*, made of deerskin.

"Put them over your boots," he said. "No bloodhound will follow you with them on. They hide the scent, and while you put them on I will tell you something."

stocking

"This is the most secret place in the forest. Men have come here to hide for many a year. When I first came here they were very poor, dressed in deer skins and living on deer's meat. That was no good to me. I wanted money; so I began selling venison."

"There are many men in Shaston and round about who will pay good money for a piece of venison and not ask where it came from. The job was to get it to them. You would laugh if I told you all the ways we have tried. But the faggots were the best. We got it out with the waggons. Has your father ever told you he is a rich man? Well, he is."

"Now that is *finished.* Well, well, we will find another way just as good, later on. Now you get back to your father and tell him to put his faggots on the waggon *as usual* to-morrow."

"Put the faggots on? Mr Perron said . . ."

"Perron is *not as good a head as* some of us, lad. Of course you must put the faggots on, the same as last time. You tell your father the faggots will be all right."

---

finished, they could not do it any more.
as usual, as he always does.
not as good a head as, not as clever as.

"You mean – there will be nothing inside?"

"You must get along home," was all Pat would say. "You ought to be in bed."

They got up.

"Walk close to me and don't speak," said Pat. Then he gave a low call, which was answered in the wood. A few minutes passed. Then Hugh heard that men were moving round him. They came up to Pat in the darkness and a few words were said. Then Pat walked on, holding Hugh by the arm, the others following behind.

They moved along paths, turning this way and that, till they found themselves where Hugh had stood that morning with his father. What a long time ago it seemed! From there he knew his way well enough.

"Off with you, lad," said Pat kindly, and Hugh went. Already men were busy round him, carrying faggots away.

It was getting light when Hugh reached the cottage door. He was just able to tell his father what had happened, but he fell asleep as he talked and he could not answer half old Maundy's questions. His mother warmed *blankets* and put them round him, and his father carried him up the ladder to the attic. He was asleep almost before he was in bed.

It was late in the afternoon when he woke up. He turned over and through the *trap-door* in the floor he saw his father's head appear.

"Boy," he said, "the foresters came this morning when we were loading Perron's waggon."

"What happened?"

"Great sport! They must have followed him on the way up, because when we had got the load on, six of them closed round us. One had his face *bandaged* and another was walking with a stick. I think they were your two friends. 'Take that load off', said one of them. Now you should have seen Perron. He just said nothing while they took the load off; and there sure enough were the faggots. 'What is this?' they said. 'Firewood,' said Perron. 'No,' they said, 'open it!' 'Open it yourselves,' said Perron. Well, they did. They opened every one, and there was nothing but sticks in any of them. 'And now,' said Perron when they had opened the last one, 'if you know what a faggot is made of will you please do them all up again and load my waggon?' He sat there and laughed and made them do it. It was the best thing I have seen for many a year."

Suddenly he stopped.

bandage

"Here I am talking while your dinner is getting cold."

He gave Hugh the food. Hugh ate some of it and looked at his father.

"What is this, father?"

"Forest mutton," said his father. Then, when he saw Hugh laugh, he laughed too.

"Don't laugh at me, lad. And don't you do anything like this again. You are going to Blandford. I am sorry, but it is a good job,

and you would have to go away for a bit to keep out of the way of the foresters. The *trade* is finished. There will be no more venison trading for many a year. Let the deer alone. Live poor and honest like – other people. And keep clear of that *devil*, Pat."

---

trade, buying and selling.

devil, bad person.

Hugh said nothing; but he remembered Pat's voice last night when he said: "Well, well, we will find another way just as good, later on."

He knew that some day he would see Pat again.

Questions

1. Where did Hugh and his family live?
2. How did Hugh get the bees out of the old man's hair?
3. Who was Pat?
4. What did Pat teach Hugh?
5. What is Dead Man's Bottom and who lived there?
6. Who was Perron?
7. What did Perron get from the wood?
8. Why did Hugh come all the way to Shaston?
9. What happened in the street?
10. How did Hugh get away from the foresters?
11. Who helped Hugh when he came to Dead Man's Bottom?
12. Why was Hugh going to Blandford and what was he going to do there?